THE COLOR
OF
WORDS

DELILAH E. AVERY GREEN

Copyright © 2022 Delilah E Avery Green
Published by Leftwich Press, Inc.
Saint Albans, NY 11412

ISBN 979-8-218-14565-1 (paperback)
Library of Congress Control Number (LCCN): 2023902027

Printed in The United States of America

DEDICATION

I dedicate this book to my late son Darryl Claude Green

ACKNOWLEDGMENTS

Number one on this list is surely, my Lord and Savior, Jesus Christ, the guiding force in my life and the giver of all good things.

To all of my family, especially my son and daughter, I thank, appreciate, and love you.

To the rest of you special folk, let it be known that all compliments, and every encouraging word was indelibly printed on my heart and acted as a catalyst for me to move forward with my dream of holding a book that my mind created.

To all of my extraordinaire relatives who have gone beyond the veil of tears, I thank you posthumously for your many words of encouragement. These include my son, parents, grandparents, aunts, uncles and cousins. Their spirits are listening.

To my relatives who still support me, this has been our venture because I would never have done it without you. I really lucked out when family members were issued.

To my friends, those of you who read the book because I wrote it, to those of you who were just curious, to those of you who heard the same poem three ways and told me each one was 'good', and to my classmates who lived long enough to share my joy; I have truly been covered by the umbrella of love - GOD BLESS YOU ALL.

To Mrs. Wanza Leftwich, an accomplished publisher, writer, and a true Christian lady. You made it happen. Thank you, with sincere appreciation and lots of love.

Table of Contents

Poetry

Poetry is my blank canvas
A shimmering crimson red
I paint on it the words I feel
That saturate my head

Poetry is the appendage to my soul
It dictates my spiritual flow
Where love in all its splendor
Gives life its ethereal glow

Poetry is my staff of life
Where ideas are spoon-fed
The recipe for my poems
Become my creative bread

Poetry fine-tunes my verbal senses
A mind innovator and my passion
Challenging the expression of my thought
Presented in my own unique fashion

Poetry is the eye of the storm
The center of the rolling wheel
The sum total of life's experiences
Encompassing everything I do, I think, I feel

Books

B ooks lined up neatly, like soldiers
Peer back as I browse the shelves
Between the pages hidden secrets
Where people express themselves

Books take me on a literary trip
Rollercoaster fast or turtle slow
The mood of the reader determines the speed
And the writer the places we go

It's a mental journey that I take
And no matter what the reader's intent
What I receive from the pages
Depends on how I interpret the print

Writer's Block

Thoughts run through my mind like dancing elves at play
I'm desperate to catch them, but none of them will stay
A masterpiece of thought lurks in my anxious mind
My thoughts run the gamut but not one verse I find
Like flies my thoughts do swarm, they buzz inside my head
Upon my creative mind they prey
But all brainwork seems dead

Creating Verse

Thoughts swirl around in my head
I dare not harness them, I must simply wait
They are joined by pleasant thoughts and memories too
They are all on one accord now, I feel I might create

I grab a bag of memories and thoughts
Emerging from the darkness to the light
I sit down and shuffle them
Now I begin to write

Colors

I used to think that
Life was either black or white
If something was not wrong
Then surely it was right

Oh, wait I see more colors
I see so many hues
Oranges, reds, yellows, browns
And several shades of blues

Colors represent variables
Because choices do abound
And though there is one problem
Several answers can be found

Red and yellow reflect experiences
And how justice has been dealt
And greys and black have determined
The joy or pain I felt

Shades of blues have taught me
How to love and not to hate
Life's lessons have taught me
That there's room to tolerate

Right and wrong sometimes intertwine
And the two seem to be entangled
But follow your conscience and you see
That right will escape untangled

Challenges

Challenges are certain things
    We feel we could do without
    But how can we learn our strengths
Unless we are thrown about

Why would a bird assume he cannot fly
Unless he has fluttered his wing
How does he know he has a voice
If he has never attempted to sing

There would be no marathons
If no challenges were met
No training and no running
No worry and no fret

Challenges are that subtle push
We need to meet a goal
The beauty of accomplishment
Is to feel success unfold

Choices

Days, months, then comes years
They all pass so swiftly now
There are doors still I need to open now
There is still so much knowledge to devour

Past, present, and my future
Neatly tied in a memory knot
Past actions, deeds, and wishes
Evolve like a serial plot

When I analyze this plot
And the choices that I've made
In the perpetual school of life
Have I made a passing grade

I fantasize about the road
That I chose not to trod
Would I have fulfilled my dreams
Or would they be trampled in the sod?

Worry

Worry creeps into my mind
And shoves all reality out
When I am feeling positive
He sprinkles thought with doubt

Worry can be very painful
And causes mental drain
While the sun is shining brightly
Worry forecasts lots of rain

Worry steals the pleasure
From my current blissful state
It tells me that my life holds
A new twist to my fate

Worry is a hurting thing
That creates imaginary grief
I wonder how to shake this fiend
And get me some relief

Worry is counterproductive
It is an addition that I abhor
But trying hard to break it
Causes me to worry even more

Discontent

I truly appreciate sweet summer
While I'm caught in winter's grip
I long for summer slushes
While now hot tea I sip

I admire the falling snowflakes
As they twirl and hit the ground
I'd trade each one for butterflies
And watch color flit around

Winter burns my eyes and face
It chaps and toughens lips
I worry should I chance to fall
I could break arms or hips

Winter dress is so cumbersome
The coat, the hat, the scarf
I dream of dress much simpler
As I dine out on the wharf

Now here it is hot summer
I'm bathed in blistering heat
I long for winters snowflakes
Then snow cream I could eat

Change

C hange is the refreshing breeze
That blows through each life
Like breezes, it can be calm or destructive
Sometimes change throws me into a stage of stagnation
Before I can emerge as the beneficiary of it

My imagination could not have believed
Or conceived in a time long past
Being a part of such drastic change
Sometimes change makes me want
To run back and snuggle in the lap of mother time

Sometimes I feel the change has sent the whole world
On a marathon race
While I am casually sauntering along
Most are passing the finish
I hope I will be able to catch up

Change is inevitable, some forced, some self-made
Some rigid and some flexible
Change reconstructs our dreams and lifestyle
Acceptance of, or refusal of
Determines many of our life goals

Even though I do not agree with many changes
Like the majority I get sucked in by them
Changes can be subtle or blatant
Shoving you backwards or forward
Once you master change your life will change immensely

Dreaming

My most productive dreaming
Is done while I'm awake
My thoughts sometimes intertwine
The real mixed with the fake

This untangling phase
Really challenges my mind
But usually with concentration
Both thoughts just then unwind

Fantasizing

I wish that I could write
The beautiful sceneries in my brain
The colors dance around so speedily
Like the rushing of a train
Wish that I could store
The sunset in all its glory
If I could put it to verse
It would be one classic story

God

W ho causes the sun to rise and the same to set
And causes the sun to dry and sends the rain to wet
Who draws in the sunshine and drapes us with night
And hung each star, a twinkling miracle bright
Who streaks the sky with lightning, and sends the thunders roar
Who channels the rushing waters lashing at the oceans shore
Who wakes me up each morning from the wondrous world of sleep
Who forms each tiny teardrop when I have cause to weep
Who created all things living, in water, land, and sea
Who gave each life a purpose and an appointed time to die

Existence

Have you ever wondered
About our privilege to exist
And if we had never arrived
Would we have been missed

But we never had a choice
So, we waited in a nothingness state
Finally rescued from oblivion
And yanked from the stage of wait

Maybe destiny facilitated our entry
And like putty we needed molding
We try to carve a niche in life
Like a rose, our bud of life unfolding

But oh, too soon we leave this place
And from this life be free
The rose is rejuvenated next season
Unlike the rose, what becomes of you and me?

God is Near

I've never really seen God, but he touches me each day
He wakes me up from sleep so sound, and listens while I pray
I have never really seen God but his majestic beauty I behold
As I watch the regal peacock strut around so bold
I see him in the mighty oak that from an acorn grew
I see him as I feel the grass and reflect upon the dew
I hear him when the thunder roars, as lightening streaks the sky
I see him in each snowflake as they slowly flutter by
I see him in the children's faces, as they wear smiles so bright
I feel him in the days end comes, as I surrender myself to sleep
I know that he is watching me as a good shepherd watches sheep

Fate

Fate, could I have a word with you
I acknowledge you as a force
But how much influence do you really have
Upon my own life's course

How much guidance do you really give
Or do you give any at all
Could you have removed the brick
Before I had the fall

Fate, I think you really do exist
I'm just not sure of the reason
And do you change as time goes on
Just like the changing seasons

Fate I'm still a bit confused
I really do not misunderstand
I just need a little clarity, please
About your relationship to man

Gut Feelings

Gut feelings are those little thoughts that scratch at my mind
There seems to be some caution, of some mysterious kind
They make me feel that there is some underlying cause
Not rush into whatever, I should just sort of pause
It gives me the feeling to keep an open eye
But all of the time I am searching for a "why"

Gut feelings just plant that little subtle doubt
That whatever the situation it just might not work out
Gut feelings do not force
Lets you hang with your own rope
Then sit back and watches, just how you chose to cope
I now do not question, I listen intently, and heed
I realize my desires might conflict with the need

Black Lives Matter

W e are a nation of racial diversity.
Embedded in the core of our creed
The viper of prejudice has alienated us
Reformation, right now an urgent need

Others have walked in shoes of oppression
And prejudice has them pinned to a wall
Our fight has always been continuous -
Fighting still - oppressions call

Just because our plight has been shared
And others have joined in our plight
We must all lift high the banner of courage
Never wavering, just fight, fight, fight

Hence, we chant black lives matter
And it is a shame we must so designate
But as long as there is sanctioned prejudice
All victims of abuse…must congregate!

Hurricane Michael Vigil

This unrelenting wrath of nature
Has wreaked havoc in its wake
Plummeting scores of folks in darkness
Putting land and limb at stake

Small vegetation sorely battered
Small cars like toothpicks thrown
It ripped the homes and flooded streets
No mercy has it shown

Does nature have a vendetta?
Or it craves manifestation of power
By unleashing fury not seen before
We wait the fearful hours

I am cowering on the couch
Awaiting the roof to take flight
I wondered what my shelter would be
I cringed and though of my plight

It was the king of known hurricanes
Even uprooted monstrous trees
It seems as though its seeing eye
Has bought man to his knees

And while man is on his knees
May he utter a sincere prayer
That he will someday understand
The force that brought him there

Hurricane Sandy

The storm is raging wildly now, I am in a panic state
I cry, I rock, I pray, and then I wait
Nature seems so terribly angry as she spews torrential rain
The trees were tossed about like feathers, and the winds spoke such disdain

There I cowered on the sofa, abject terror now my lot
My life seems to hang in the balance, would I survive or would I not
Winds so forceful that the house shook, from the roof right to the floor
Expecting entrance any minute as the winds slammed against the door

Howling winds that seemed so desolate, drowning out my pounding heart
Surely angels will camp around me, praying that a host take part
When Sandy had finished with her fury, she calmly left without fanfare
Leaving disaster in her wake, mass destruction everywhere

Now I soaked up the quietness and surveyed the brand-new day
A miracle just witnessed, I reflect, I rejoice, I pray.

Covid 2020

L ife is so different and taxing
   Changing drastically overnight
   It seems the world we used to know
Is now replaced with hate and fright

It seems calmness and serenity
No longer now exist
With death and suffering galore
How long will this plague persist

We go about our usual task
While the mask of gloom is worn
Tranquility is almost extinct
So much pain has been borne

But we still will press onward
Reaching for relief tomorrow
Praying fervently for some change
Seeing solace from this sorrow

Mask Power – 2020

Where are the unmasked smiles
The spontaneity of a hug, a kiss
The abandonment of utter joy
These things I certainly miss

I miss conversing without concern
And wondering who chose to vaccinate
I feel so uptight and alone
I almost choose to tempt fate

My mask is the symbol of bondage
I'm tired and I yearn to be free
But I have to think of others
While hoping they do likewise for me

I miss the freedom of feeling safe
When I grasp another's hand
I miss the casualness of existence
I feel as tight as a rubber band

I miss the freedom of moving about
Without feeling life has been compromised
I hate the death of so many people
It seems so senseless through mortals' eyes

Although things seem desolate right now
I feel the bond with humanity is strong
As the world now uses their eyes to smile
I trust it is a mere question of how long?

Loneliness

L oneliness is a state of mind
Felt frequently in a crowd
Though dancers sway around me
With good music blasting loud

Though the tunes are happy ones
And everyone pats their feet
I am so somber and removed
I stay glued right to my seat

The loneliness engulfs me
As people sway in twos
The happier they seem to be
The more I have the blues

My body is in attendance
But my thoughts now dwell afar
I try to blank out lover's face
As I rise to seek the bar

Let Me Console You

W ill you let me console you
Cradle you in an outstretched arm
May each word that I speak
Act as a swiftly soothing balm

Will you let me share your pain
Basked in loves united powers
Locked in body, mind, and spirit
Where each moment transcends hours

Will you let me walk beside you
Minds in tuned and hands entwined
One main force, two souls walking
Memories dancing through their minds

Will you let me love you fiercely
Wildly as the rivers rush
Constant as the rising sun
Sweeter than an angel's blush

Nothing

I fluff up my pillow, pull the draperies closed, and turn off the television
As I prepare to relax
Yes, takes some preparation to do it properly
I immediately erase all of the day's activity from my mind
Thoughts of what tomorrow brings are expunged
And yesterday's memories get trampled in the mud of time

I will not indulge my palate by eating or drinking
My phone gets turned off
Languishingly stretch my body out on the couch
No soft music to disturb this tranquil state
I am now completely indulged in the sheer ecstasy of doing absolutely nothing

My Family Tree

I watched the leaves flutter down
Like scholars leaving home
To make their fortune, some return
But most just choose to roam
The pine tree represents family
Dignity, the pine stands tall
Now and then a cone drop
A member heeds death's call
Then I notice that it's sap time
And the sap drips down the side
It reminds me of family DNA
That our family shares with pride
Now all the scholars have gone away
But we are limbs of the same tree
Like pinecones cluster
We are bonded together to be free

My Prize

All plants I grow are special
I feed them and I toil
Watering, seeding, and planting
And buying rich, nutritious soil

Such a plant was my tomato
I watched my prize tomato with glee
The first and largest tomato
Was always picked and eaten by me

Twas the beauty of the harvest
Although I did enjoy the taste
I nurtured each plant well
And could not tolerate waste

Today I check the tomato's size
And the vibrant shade of red
I started to pick it and eat it
But decided to wait instead

Tomorrow will be better
I'll catch it at dawn
I'll sit on the back step and eat it
And feed peanuts to squirrels on the lawn

Today, today my tomato I will eat
So succulent, red, and sweet
Alas I nearly stumbled
Half-eaten prize beneath my feet

Skywatching

W hile I lay here gazing skyward, heaven and I connect
I lie motionless and watch as the billowing clouds
dissect
An extravaganza of movement of mesmerizing forms
displayed
True works of art hung high, abstract, and disarrayed
Forms float and entangle, then separate at will
They come in a thousand sizes, the epitome of skill
Different forms appear so vividly, then they fade from view
Where you saw one object, it now becomes two
As I gaze in awe, my thoughts take flight in space
I feel a part of me transcend while I lie here in place
This show is never cancelled, no collection at the door
Just lift your eyes to heaven, showtime is evermore

Internet Dating

The internet is a wondrous tool
That reaches far and wide
People many miles away
Come swiftly to your side

People that you'd never meet
Now visit you each day
You invite them into your life
Some will be transient, some stay

But the internet will never replace
The interchange of a date
And only time will weed out
Those not destined by fate

Where chemistry might exist
The internet cannot convey
There must be physical contact
There's just no other way

And should there be no sparks
And no palpations of the heart
Then friendship can prevail
From an internet start

Hugs

S ome hugs bring delightful squeals of joy
Abandonment of the moment, swallowed up
You identify this guy most assuredly
As you watch a child romp with a pup

Some hugs just say nice to meet you
They are the most reserved kind
These are given very guardedly
Like the sharing of fine wine

Some hugs just scream out, "Please stay!"
They plead don't leave me like this
Check out the face on the kindergarten child
As she holds her mother by the wrist

Some hugs say, "Welcome home!"
You've been gone such a long time
Just give me a hug and rest yourself
You're here and now life is prime

Some hugs say, "Do I have to right, now?"
My friends are looking this way
I'm ten and I love my dear Aunt Lucie Ray
But don't let her kiss me, I pray

Some hugs speak of feelings of remorse
Very repentance and oh so contrite
They just need a hug of forgiveness
Now all can sleep well through the night

Some hugs are filled with loving passion
And declarations of love and bliss
This is seen when loving couples

Seal their married vows with a kiss

Hugs are so private, yet universal
And they are seldom misunderstood
Even in the worst of bad times
A hug feels really feels quite good!

If

If you were a rainbow, you would the pot of gold
And I would be the color so vibrant and so bold
And if you were an apple, you would be the core
And if you were a game, you would be the highest score
And if you were a season, you surely would be spring
You would even be the sunshine, the lovely flowers bring
And if you were a playing card, you surely would be ace
You'd be the crossing line if I should win the race
And if you were a road a turnpike you would be
And there beside the turnpike, that sideroad would be me

Love Is

L ove is a raging wildfire, fanned by the flame of passion
Where burning love leaves behind, smoldering embers in
the ashes
Love is like a gentle touch as kissed by a summer breeze
As elusive as the birds that dart among the trees
Love is the spice of life that give your life its flavor
The epitome of happiness, a world of memories savor
Love is the fulfillment of dreams, where hearts become entwined
It is the embodiment of ecstasy where raw emotions are defined`

Love

L ove is stronger than steel
And as fragile as steam
Can be a heartwarming experience
Or a smasher of dreams

Love is the heat of human kindness
That makes our heart feel light
Handle with care and compassion
Misuse could induce its flight

Love comes from so many directions
Lovers, friends, family, every source
Some rain of love showers over us
No matter what life's course

So, enjoy love in all its flavors
And cherish it with concern
Whether it be casual and sweet
Or hot enough to burn

Love is simply showing kindness
That is thrown and then comes back
Good to give and good to receive
Once it's gone you suffer a lack

My Conscious

The quiet time, the still of the night
My feelings freely flow
No words, just thoughts abide
New ideas born, now grow

The rigors of a fruitful day
Now stilled by fall of night
Time to attend to inner thoughts
So peaceful and contrite

The silence seems a blanket
With which I wrap my soul
Reflective thoughts breed future plans
Time to access each goal

These moments go uncluttered
My spirit dances free
It's in these cherished moments
My conscious lectures me

Morning Wonder

W ith hope in my heart and a spade in my hand
    I gently toil in the earth
    Although spring comes back every year
Each return heralds the rebirth

The digging of the virgin soul
Is a sign of resurrection
In this spot where now, I kneel
Will bloom flowers of perfection

New birds make nests in the same tree
Then someday the tree will die
But always when you look around
Eternal beauty fills the sky

Spring bursts forth into a new life
That winter temporarily halted
Draped in beauty unexcelled
The wonder of God exalted

How

How do the birds without compasses
Find their destination in flight
And how do the tiny fireflies
Choose to light up the night
How does the beautiful butterfly
Know when to exit the cocoon
And how does a newborn baby
Determine when to leave the womb?

Snow

I stare out my living room window
And watch snow drift quietly down
No matter how much swirling is done
Flakes fall without the benefit of sound

Snow establishes the criteria for whiteness
And each snowflake seems to comply
And though I have watched many snowflakes
I've never seen a dingy one float by

Snow has a certain calming quality
That spreads over my entire being
It seems so calming and blissful
Watching sends all stress fleeing

The purity and serenity snow evokes
Catapults me into a spiritual sphere
Where the miracle of nature embraces earth
And the majesty of nature becomes clear

But life too like snow is everchanging
Like the snowflakes, we are tossed around
Do we remain fragile like they
Or have we learned to bounce off the ground

My Mind

My mind is like a giant sieve
That filters out all matter
The stuff deemed unimportant
Gets trashed as worthless data

My mind is like a racehorse
That travels at high speed
So much for it to process
Each thought, action, and deed

My mind is like a receptacle
For all my brain's intake
Both works diligently and non-stop
Whether sleeping or awake

My mind is an accumulation
Of all I do, think, or process
A conglomeration of good and bad
Of sorrow and happiness

My mind is like a newspaper
My personality is the print
The story that it truly tells
Is how my life is spent

Who Are We

We are a race of noblemen
Of peasants, queens, and kings
We are the very essence
Of which our anthems sing

We are a race of pioneers
Struggles fraught with tears
With perseverance and hard work
Still struggling over the years

We are a race of many hues
As varied as a kaleidoscope
We are a race of strengths
We are a race of hope

We are a race of spiritual beings
We live our lives with passion
Our dress reflects our style of life
As seen through the eyes of fashion

We are a race of intellects
Constant changes we embrace
We are a compilation of mankind
We are the human race

The Symbol

Tattered clothes and shackled feet, separated families, dignity
stripped
Torn brutally from our homeland, for any reason, brutally
whipped
Women ravished, men sold, like commodities on the street
Food was only leftover fare, still, they bowed to no defeat

I can see their eyes flash anger, and their lips pursed tight with hate
Praying fervently, while being beaten, when will these assaults
abate
Their religious beliefs sustained, while they endured so much
wrong
But they looked to a higher plane and created spirituals as their
song

It is because they shed those tears, while they pulled the cotton
sack
It is because their fighting spirit could not be bloodied like their
back
Freedom was a constant dream, that festered like a leaking sore
But they created an escape plan, to live that way, no more, no more

Slavery was our country's blight, that will be in history
forevermore
Like a shiny, golden apple, that was rotted to the core
I was not there when they hung you, but I can still flinch from the
pain

I was not there when they sold you, but the memories never wane
Ancestors it is because you lived, that today I can hope
That never again will our nation have a symbol
That dangles from the end of a rope

Political Statement

Most people think our country is racing downward in a
hurry
It's in distress it's plain to see and could be cause for
worry
Innocent kids being threatened by adults and their peers
Need more awareness and counseling to work through their fears
No wonder some kids lack direction and some even bully their
peers
Our taxes are still rising like a river, how soon will relief be in
sight
Homeowners losing their homes, who is responsible for this plight
Some politicians seem to forget, just who gave them their vote
And act on the things promised from the flowery speeches they
wrote
Apathy is a national disease, and yes, it's quite contagious
This malady is like a poisonous snake that coils and lies in wait
By the time we realize we've been bitten, it already is then too late

What Does It Mean

What does it mean to be safe
To be able to have dignity and worth
To have an inalienable right to life
By the very nature of your birth

What does it mean to be free
To be able to hold your head high
To be able to enjoy your birthright
And get an equal piece of the pie

What does it mean to be afraid
Though right was your intent
To be the victim of abuse for naught
Makes you wonder where equality went

What does it mean to be American
Not quite the land of the free
Our forefathers had good intentions
But they haven't always worked for me

Sitting in a Dark Room

Darkness, darkness I abhor you
You seem so hard, cold, and unfeeling
Being in your presence depresses me
Sending taunt emotions reeling

Stealthily you creep upon me
And surround me like puffs of smoke
I see various mysterious reflections
Feel your aura like devil's smoke

Everything seems so distorted
As you invade my private space
I can only glean the shadows
Not discerning my own face

Darkness, darkness you engulf me
Making chills go up my spine
Day is breaking, you must leave now
Peace of day will soon be mine

Something is Wrong

My senses are really confused
A negative presence here I feel
My nerves seem strangely raw
They are usually made of steel
I suspect there could be something wrong

It is in the way you kiss
Now reduced to a quick peck
Whatever happened to the real kiss
And the way you'd nuzzle my neck
Could there be something wrong?

It is in the way that I'm greeted
Makes me feel less desired
I know you work long hours
But you seem more bored than tired
Are you sure there is nothing wrong?

Your work is now all-consuming
No scheduled family time
Brings memories of a yesterday
When all we did was prime
I truly suspect something is wrong

The telephone call that ended
The minute I entered the room
Another wrong number, like the others
Is that what I am supposed to assume
Will you tell me right now what is wrong?

The presence of a faceless ghost
Looms over our marital bliss
Inequities of this magnitude

I choose not to dismiss
We can no longer pretend nothing's wrong

The presence of another love
Creates a chasm wide
Like a rhinoceros in our room
It's far too large to hide
Something is most definitely wrong

Survival

O h, what a gorgeous day it is now
I now face my assortment of pills
The only task that I hate even more
Is paying my huge stack of bills

When I feel a little sluggish
I took a brand-new cure for that
Only to find later
That it stole my belly fat

I am afraid of brittle bones
If I should fall and break my hip
I fear it would be the end of me
From just that one small slip

So, I take a pill to harden bones
This cause digestion some duress
I feel slightly overwhelmed
Bring on my pill for stress

Taste buds too have gone awry
I do not have much definitive taste
Hope the pink pill works for that
Too much food now I waste

When I became a senior
My health developed brand new issues
Sinus and an allergy or too
I should buy stock in Kleenex tissues

I can move around now freely
And I remember most folks' names
As long as I can arise each day
I am happy to be playing in life's game

Thoughts of You

Thoughts of you recharge my zest for life
Like a brand-new battery in a new machine
Lifts my spirits as though I was rescued
From the bottom of a dark ravine
Thinking about you comforts and soothes me
Covers me with a blanket of peace
Your voice whispers so tenderly
And speaks of a love without cease

The Shade

My shade of life was lifted
The day that I was born
Another humble child of fate
To greet the welcoming dawn
Sometimes my shade reflects sunlight
And the beams shine like dew
It is then I'm in a happy place
And my worries then are few
On gloomy days it shows the storm
When all things seem amiss
But when it's raised in brighter times
I then enjoy the bliss
Transparent is my life shade
I can see clearly out or in
It reflects where I am going
And shows where I have been
Through each season of my life
There is the lowering of the shade
And when I reach the fall
The light begins to fade
There is now the vacant window
Where the shade had been
This is now the winter of my life
And now all seasons end

Sulking

T ell me what I did
       To make you so upset
       I wonder what it was
To offend you so, my pet

Was it something that I did
Or something I forgot
Or something that I should
And I did what I should not

Was I supposed to leave
And I decided to stay
Or are you being ornery
And just want to have your way

We'll never get this settled
If you don't do your part
Just speak right up and tell me
What you feel inside your heart

Oh no, I get it now, back turned
You do not care to converse
Lying under blanket with covered head
Only serves to make it worse

And then he flipped the covers
And shot me a sheepish grin
I didn't hear a word you said
I had my earplugs in

The Affair

Cheating takes away my spirit while doing the best I can
While dealing with reality, I have to share the man
It takes away the knowledge that he will ever be true
The relationship is shortchanged when it's being shared by two
It's the sneaking on the backstreet, avoiding confrontation should
we
Meet see the real object of his affection, requires us to be discreet
Most holidays and weekends, I'm destined to be alone
I'm not allowed the privilege of calling his home phone
I cannot feel very special, my ego drags the floor
I should use my common sense and bar him from my door
One should only need one person to fan their flame of passion
Only one should be quite ample if done in proper fashion
It's like getting one slice when I desire the whole loaf of bread
It's really playing dangerous mind games that play inside my head
I battle with my conscious, to end this dead-end tryst
I know he has another, how much will I be missed
His calls have become less frequent, mine seldom receive a reply
Somehow there lurks the feeling that a break-up could be nigh
While traveling to the dentist, in pain and body weary
There right before my eyes, my love, and his new dearie
We exchanged brief hellos, my body in a trance
They stroll right past me without a backward glance
His eyes were piercingly cold
Who was that I heard her say
Just someone I used to know
My heart just walked away

Symphony

The song is poetry set to music, and since I dare not try to sing
I delve into poetry to hear that melodious ring
It flaps into the atmosphere like the wings of birds, but higher
Music is the mixture of my thoughts, that dance, and play
It sets my soul to break loose, lets my imagination stray
I listen to the symphony that is plays within my head
It is the lullaby I sing, that lingers long after bed
It is the realm of wonder and the patter of my feet
It is the marching band that struts along the street
The symphony of music is the embellishment of sound
My heart beats to the rhythm as my body twirls around

The Cardinal

I stared through my back door,
on the railing beautiful and bold
Sat a majestic, beautiful cardinal

I waited for this scenario to unfold
His head cocked aside as to greet me
Small beady eyes darted in his head

I wanted to feed him but he'd, fly away,
So, I remained quiet instead
His feathers were such a magnificent hue,

To the touch, they would be silky and soft
Maybe like the finest of silk,
Or some other magnificent cloth

I was intrigued by his seemingly large size,
Now that he was no longer in a tree
I watched him very quietly,

Piercing eyes seemed to be judging me
I tried to drink in all the beauty
Of such a breathtaking creature

Close up more gorgeous than I imagined,
Now that I could clearly see each feature
And when he decided to take flight,

I wondered what his perception was of me
I was probably a strange-looking captive, caged.
And wishing desperately to be free

The Harmonica

We sat quietly on the back step
Born three generations apart
We connected by his special gift
Of playing music from his heart

My grandpa then was fifty-nine
And I was just nine years old
He'd play the harp so hauntingly
The blues played funky and bold

He seemed to transcend time
As he lost himself in play
Back to a real blue time
His own life of yesterday

And then he'd play a happy tune
And we would pat our feet
And all the kids would gather round
The music sounding sweet

Whenever I hear a harmonica
I truly delight in its sound
My mind rocks to and fro
Where fond memories now abound

The Jitters

I gaze upward as midnight makes its run
It is now the pre-dawn of activity
I stare out the window sleepily
Did I hear a noise outside or has my imagination run amuck?
The whole world seems to be on lock-down
Even the streetlight seems dim and useless
The window is cracked open, and I inhale the breeze
I am here alone
Things that look so familiar in the glare of the sun,
Take on distorted shapes by the fear of the night
I find quietness very disconcerting, yet foreign sounds startle me
Not one car has passed, the streets seem strangely desolate
The stars and moon seem further away
I wrap my arms around myself and shudder
I bang the window closed and lock it
Again, I try to embrace sleep

Where the Wind Blows Free

My senses romp and play and bask in the freedom
I sense a hush that speaketh not
I am awed by feeling what I cannot see
I feel as naked as an alpaca shorn of his fleece
The exhilaration of the free blowing wind
Catapults my mind into a force of mystery
Where the wind blows free without end

Unfilled Dreams

I will run out of precious time
Well before I fulfill my dreams
I still plan and wait for fruition
Formulating plans, goals, and schemes

I have so many unfilled dreams
They bombard me with ideas
To fulfill them all sufficiently
I'd need another fifty years

Never will I finish
All the dreams that I create
I'll leave behind unfinished ones
I know that will be my fate

When my dreaming ends
Unfilled dreams will not die
I'll cut them up in pieces
And drop them from the sky

I'll watch them as they descend
And slowly drift apart
But I pray my unfilled dreams
Find a life in another heart

Delilah E. Avery Green

The Mirror of Life

Today I took a good look in life's mirror
I saw the same world of yesteryear
However so much had been added as I looked
Now the whole world is riveted with fear

I go about with some semblance of sanity
But underneath the façade, deep regret
That a birthright of quality is still a dream
And those who still say, not yet

I took another look, and I felt the pain
Of thousands who marched before
Injustice rampant on every hand
People getting tired now say, no more

Still observing life's mirror
Every conceivable color and creed
Humanity marching in unison
Equality, their one basic need

As I continue to stare at the mirror
My expectations and home seem deflated
It shows more chaotic situations ahead
Unless this storm of violence can be abated

Memories

Memories rush my subconscious
Like a subtle sneak attack
Like the sturdiness of a dam
That keeps holding rivers back

Memories keep floating
In the surface of my mind
They are such pleasant memories
Of the secondary kind

Memories are formed
Via the life that we have led
They collect and store the data
From which our thoughts are fed

Memories are our connection bond
That has held our minds intact
We make more each day we live
They are the present sailing back

Tribute to My Mom
The Late Naomi Boone Avery Robinson

S he taught me to harness work
And to hitch it to my dream
She told me to remember
Things are not always as they seem

She always made each day so special
In a caring and devoted way
Shared with me religious ties.
I learned from her to pray

My mom was a special gift
And one I'll always treasure
She was the best I must confess
Understanding without measure

She was lavish with encouragement
And the first to utter praise
Wisdom sealed within my heart
That will sustain me all my days

She accepted me for who I am
Not who she wanted me to be
Her love reached to the depth of time
Like the roots of an old oak tree

She was elegant and graceful
She taught by a prime example
Wisdom slowly meted out
With a love that proved quite ample

She locked me in her heart real tight
Yet encouraged my own flight
I know she knelt in prayer
In the middle of the night

Thank you, Mom, for giving me the best you so I could someday become the best me.

My Mother's Chair

Whenever I placed my mother's chair in the corner of my room, I saw myself rocking and maybe crocheting or doing some other kind of needlework. I have not had the luxury of having enough time to either sit and watch TV and do absolutely nothing nor have I found time to do any needlework in her chair.

However, just having that chair there has become a catalyst for me to stay focused on my writing and other things that require major concentration. Sometime when I cannot stay focused, I curl up in her rocker and just ravel down memory lane and pick up pieces of the past and little scraps of nostalgia and before I realize it, I have enough bits and pieces to tie together and return to reality to write.

That empty chair has brough so much fulness and energy into my life. I think of it as my place to meditate, think, and reestablish my connections. That chair is not empty, that chair is the most productive piece of furniture in my house.

It is where my mother joins me in quiet time. It is where I rejoin her in her knitting. It is a spiritual lighting of past embers in the fire of our emotions.

The Hanger

A t a touch, the padded area feels almost human
So soft and cuddly, I brush it across my face
It once held a tiny, beautiful yellow dress
But now, an aura of nothingness in its place

My child wore that dress with happiness
And she kissed my heart with her glee
She loved to listen to stories
As we sat 'neath the old oak tree

Now there's an angel clad in yellow
That was her favorite dress
I see her frolicking it
As I hold the hanger to my breast

Many, many years have now passed
Since we bade her sad depart
But she never really left
Because she still frolics in our heart

The Solution

It is so good to see you here
So much happened since last we met
So many different and horrible things
Causing us to pause, reflect, and fret

Life is so different and taxing
Changing drastically overnight
It seems the love we seemed to have
Now replaced with hate and fright

The calmness and serenity
No longer now exist
With death and suffering galore
How long will this persist

We go about our usual task
But the mask of gloom is worn
Tranquility is almost extinct
So much pain has been borne

But we still look press onward
Holding to tomorrow
Praying fervently for some change
Seeking solace from this sorrow

As I survey the turmoil
And the limitation of man
God will give man the needed boost
To show him that he can

Time

T ime caters to the very young
Their wish is his command
He is their future and their friend
They feel that life is grand

Time cradles youth to his bosom
They doze and are quite content
Only to find when they awake
A whole life has been spent

Time is a flying boomerang
That come swiftly flying back
You think you will be old someday
But then time makes a sneak attack

Now oh so soon our future
Seems less sure and confident
We reminisce about our life
And how our time was spent

Time lulls into a sense of complacency
As though it will always be there
But it is snatched away so abruptly
That the passing of time seems unfair

Time now has no more tomorrows
He thrives on now and yesterday
What was once his dozing youth
Has now become his prey

The Mysteries of Sleep

S leep bids me leave realities clutch
　　To a place of angels, nightmares, and such
　　Sometimes sleep seems just a valley of peace
Where life's rigorous ritual cease

Sometimes I embrace him, wait his arrival
I know he is crucial to a healthy survival
But sometimes he is late, and I toss and fret
Time seems endless and he is not here yet

However, there are times he won't wait
Until I am tucked into bed
He finds me in my rocker, and I nod instead
This happens too when I'm in a crowd
And if I am fortunate, I won't snore too loud

Awareness has fled, I no longer seem to exist
As sleep totally wraps me in this mysterious tryst
Sleep transforms me into a catatonic state
There I remain till sleep deems me wake

If sleep forgot to wake me, how would I ever get back
Would I be forever suspended in a state of dread
Could I, without sleep, find my own way back to me
Or would I indeed be quite dead?

Trading Places

W ould I trade my life for yours taking all your joys and sorrow
Would I willingly exchange mine for yours tomorrow
Would I find that you have problems of which I am totally
unaware
Problems that would really make me throw my hands up in despair
Though it seems like your greener grass that looks good from where I
stand
Would upon a close inspection be intermingled with some sand
Would all the joy and happiness that seems to fill your life
Would I find it saturated with some pain and strife
Would I find that your small hill would become my mountain tall
And would I find your smooth path would cause me to slip and fall
If I walked a mile in your shoes would my feet be tired and sore
Would I want to give it all up feeling I could take no more
Since we are so very different in each hope and dream
I have come to the realization things are not always as they seem
So, I won't trade places with you, I have no idea what is your lot
Knowing life has really taught me to be satisfied with what I've got

Thank You Lord

How many times have I asked you, Lord
For things not based on need
Some of the things I requested of you
Might even be labeled as greed

How many times have I questioned you
When I've been solely stressed
Instead, I should have been thanking you
Because I am truly blessed

How many times have I questioned
When to me life seemed unfair
I should have been praising you
For all your loving care

How many times have I said, "why me"?
When things to me went awry
Instead, I should have been trusting and believing
Knowing that you are always nigh

How many times have you blessed me Lord
Even though I seemed unaware
Thank you, Lord, for your patient love
and for your infinite and constant care